Serengeti

PLAINS OF GRASS

For Rena
—L. B.

Published by
PEACHTREE PUBLISHING COMPANY INC.
1700 Chattahoochee Avenue
Atlanta, Georgia 30318-2112
PeachtreeBooks.com

Text © 2022 by Leslie Bulion
Illustrations © 2022 by Becca Stadtlander

First trade paperback edition published in 2024

Edited by Vicky Holifield
Design and composition by Adela Pons

The illustrations were created in gouache and pastels.

Printed and bound in November 2023 by
Toppan Leefung, DongGuan, China.
10 9 8 7 6 5 4 3 2 (hardcover)
10 9 8 7 6 5 4 3 2 1 (trade paperback)
HC ISBN: 978-1-68263-191-1
PB ISBN: 978-1-68263-651-0

Cataloging-in-Publication Data is available from the Library of Congress.

Serengeti
PLAINS OF GRASS

Written by **LESLIE BULION** | Illustrated by **BECCA STADTLANDER**

Ω

PEACHTREE

ATLANTA

Serengeti:
An Ecosystem in Motion

In early winter, moist monsoon winds from the Indian Ocean carry rain to the volcanic soils of the Serengeti Plain. Grasses sprout and flowers bloom, heralding the return of Earth's most spectacular migration of large mammals. More than a million western white-bearded wildebeests, hundreds of thousands of zebras, Thomson's gazelles, and other herbivores travel from the wooded hills in the north to feast on plants growing in the endless open spaces of the southern short-grass plain.

Each migrating and resident animal has its place in the complex web of the Serengeti ecosystem. Zebras graze on taller grasses, while wildebeests prefer shorter blades. These grazers must find watering holes to drink. Giraffes and the tiny antelopes known as dik-diks are browsers, getting their nutrition and water from the leaves and fruit of trees and shrubs. Gazelles are mixed feeders that can graze *and* browse.

Grazing and trampling helps new grasses and small plants grow. Large herbivores' heavy hooves also flush hordes of insects into the air. Hitchhiking birds are rewarded two ways: they eat parasites from the skins of their plant-eating host animals and snatch startled grass-dwelling insects in flight.

Carnivores like lions, cheetahs, and hyenas turn their attentions toward the herd as the great migration moves through their territories and beyond. Though these predators and others prey upon stragglers, and upon calves, foals, and fawns born on the plain, the herd's numbers remain strong. Rodents, lizards, and other small animals hide among boulder heaps called kopjes (KOP-eez).

In early spring, monsoon winds begin to shift away from the southern Serengeti Plain. Wildebeests, zebras, Thomson's gazelles, and other migrants scatter northwest, seeking greener grasses. Later in the season, the herd will gather into columns that stretch for miles toward the distant rains and permanent watering holes of the western acacia woodlands.

As they follow the rains, the animals must cross crocodile-filled rivers to reach the hilly lands farther north by summertime. When monsoon winds bring early winter rains, the herd returns to the southern short-grass plain of the Serengeti once again.

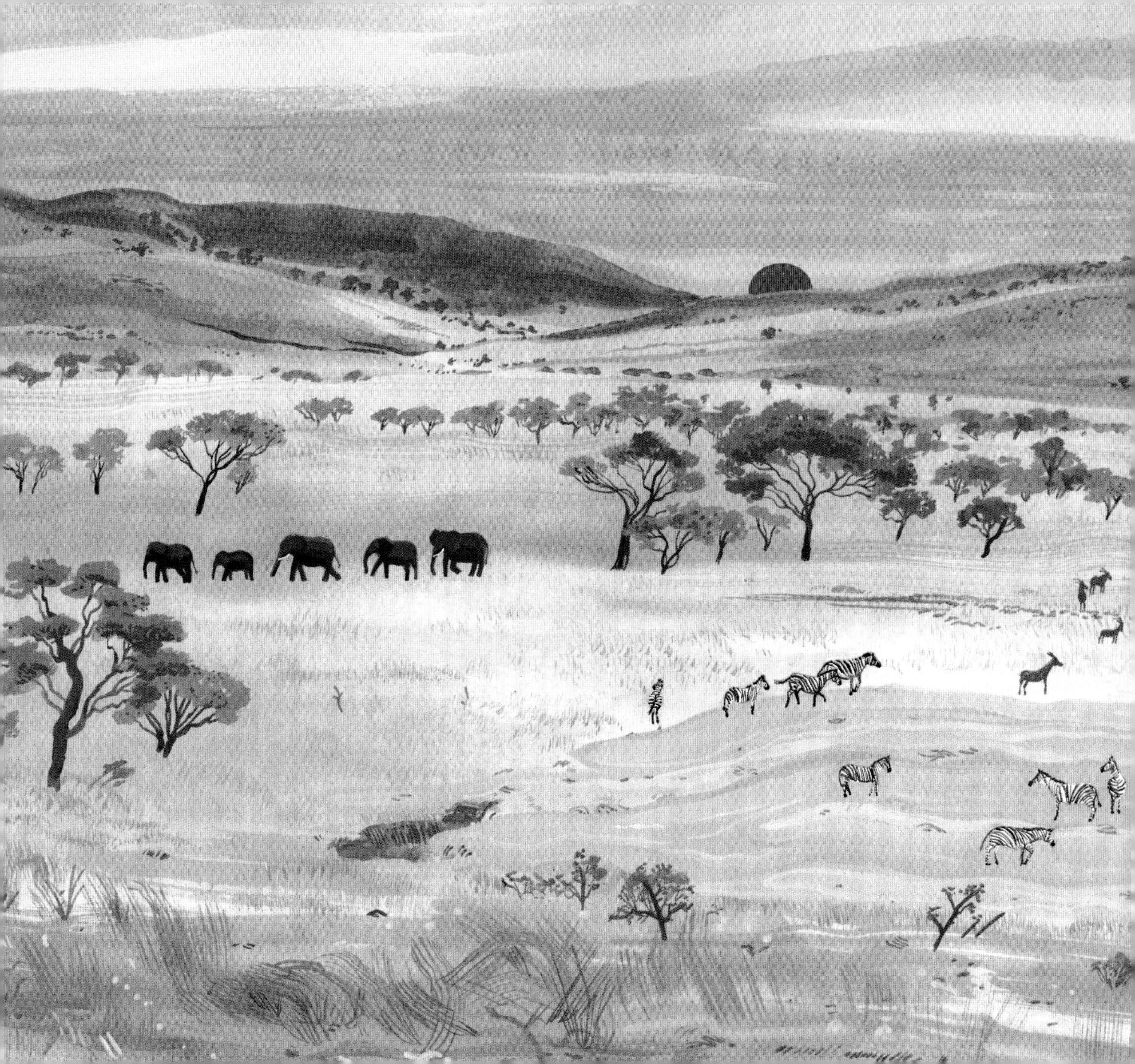

Parched soil bed of volcano ash,
roots asleep in a tangled mesh,
one drop, two, then downpour's rush,
first rains wake new blades of grass.

Tender blades of grasses die back during the dry season.
Their shallow roots are ready to send up new green shoots
when early winter rains return to Serengeti's short-grass plain.

Ancient and more recent volcanoes near Serengeti have hurled clouds of ash into the sky. As volcanic ash settles onto soil, it deposits minerals and nutrients that help plants grow.

Hoofbeats thunder under blazing sun,
a great migration toward the plain,
grazing zebras, first to begin,
clear away taller, tougher grass.

Plains zebras have sharp front teeth to cut through the tough stems and leaves of tall grasses. They get the nutrients they need by eating and quickly digesting lots of grass.

Wildebeests feast on shorter swards,
oxpecker birds are stowaboards,
gnus trample roots in shaggy herds,
spreading manure for growing grass.

Red-billed oxpeckers hitch rides on wildebeests (also called gnus) and other large plant-eating mammals. These cardinal-sized birds are known to pick ticks and other bothersome insects from the skin of their hosts. But oxpeckers also help themselves to sips of their hosts' blood by pecking at open wounds.

Wildebeests use their wide mouths to graze on short, tender grasses. They chew, swallow, spit up, then slowly chew their food a second time to get the nutrients they need.

A sward is an area of grass.

Plains are cropped where wildebeests grazed,
leaving tender herbs exposed,
low-ground growth is nimbly used,
fleet gazelles nibble gnu-mown grass.

Thomson's gazelles find tender new grasses and low-growing annual plants, also called herbs, after zebras and wildebeests have grazed a patch of the Serengeti short-grass plain.

Acacia leaf buds brush the sky,
thorns stand guard, warn: *keep away*,
lithe, rugged tongues let giraffes enjoy,
chewing cud, stilt-walking through the grass.

A Maasai giraffe safely winds its twenty-inch-long, leathery black tongue between an acacia tree's menacing spines to pluck and enjoy its tasty leaves.

Bathed by rain, Serengeti blooms,
sun-faced yellows and scarlet flames,
waste paper flowers on tiny stems,
scattered as handfuls across the grass.

Seeds of wildflowers swell and sprout, bringing splashes of color to Serengeti's grassy plains. The low-growing waste paper flower may bloom in crumpled petals of white or pink.

Butterflies flutter at nectar wells,
whistling thorns host ant patrols,
hoofed herds stir up grasshopper gales,
cattle egrets feast above the grass.

Grasshoppers eat plants, and birds and other animals eat grasshoppers, moving energy along the food web.

Stinging, biting ants protect their whistling thorn acacia homes when browsers such as young giraffes or elephants try to munch leaves.

Butterflies and other insects spread pollen from flower to flower.

Ancient boulder heaps mark the plains,
kopjes shelter hyrax clans,
rock rabbits gobble freshest greens,
dart home from perilous open grass.

Over hundreds of thousands of years, winds and rains have worn away the volcanic ash and soft soils of the Serengeti to reveal piles of very old, hard rocks called kopjes.

Furry rock hyraxes live in family groups. Keeping an eye out for predators, these "rock rabbits" eat quick meals of mostly leaves, grasses, and fruit.

Kopje's shadow, moon-washed night,
dik-diks pair in a life duet,
hind-legged stretch for leaves and fruit,
elfin hiders in the grass.

Dik-diks leave their hiding spots to browse, most often at night. Like giraffes, hyraxes, and other resident animals, these tiny antelopes don't migrate with the herd.

Mating termites ride the wind,
nest, then chew chaff underground,
workers raise mounds of clay and sand,
towers sail in a sea of grass.

Mound-building termites chew up and digest grass roots
as well as the dry husks of grains and grasses, called chaff.
Termites' wastes mix into and feed Serengeti soils.

Mounds are breached by spade-clawed swipe,
aardvark's tongue is a termite scoop,
trot to burrow as sun comes up,
thick tail trailing, bending grass.

Aardvarks use their strong, sharp claws to open termite mounds and dig burrows. Their foot-long, sticky tongues are perfect tools for capturing termites in narrow tunnels.

Abandoned mound under night's dark wing,
dawn uncoils with a flickering tongue,
hyrax flees from poisoned fang,
mamba wends through whispering grass.

Tunnels of emptied termite mounds are connected to cool underground spaces, providing naturally air-conditioned hiding spots for many Serengeti animals, including the venomous black mamba, predator of small mammals and birds.

Stalk-legged raptor, keen-eyed stroll,
scans for scurry, slither, or crawl,
secretary bird wields claw and bill,
mamba whips from cloak of grass.

Secretary birds use their beaks and stomping feet to hunt for small mammals, insects, lizards, and snakes. Outstretched wings and long, scaly legs help protect this raptor from the deadly bite of a black mamba.

Daring jackals, sly and fast,
scavenge, hunt, and rarely rest,
frogs, fruit, carrion—no meal missed,
dik-dik fawn hides in the grass.

Golden jackals are omnivores that forage, hunt, and pick over all kinds of available foods in the Serengeti, including plants, animals, and the bodies of dead animals, called carrion.

Gazelle herds grazing, striped tails flick,
tense, alert to cheetah's mark,
patient predator built to streak,
dappled earth patches in tawny grass.

A stalking cheetah's spots and tear marks keep it well camouflaged among Serengeti's grasses—until it sprints in at top speed for the kill.

Hang-gliding vultures, mid-air dives,
cackling scrum lures hyena thieves,
strong jaws leave only horns and hooves,
hungry cheetah fades into grass.

White-backed vultures glide on warm, rising air currents
and use their sharp eyesight to spot a predator killing prey.
These scavengers also follow other vultures, spiraling down
to join a noisy feeding group, or scrum.

Spotted hyenas are predators and scavengers that help keep Serengeti clean by eating animal parts (such as skin and bones) that other meat eaters can't digest. Hyenas follow vultures to their scrums and will gang up to chase off the predator that first made the kill.

Plains rolled clean of animal scat,
buried in tunneled nesting spot,
aerating soil and feeding root,
dung beetle tills its garden of grass.

Dung beetles eat fresh animal poop, also called dung, scat, or manure. Some roll dung into a tiny ball and bury it to eat later. Some lay their eggs on or in the dung ball where larvae can hatch safely and well fed. Dung beetles are busy recyclers that mix air and nutrients back into the soil of the Serengeti Plain.

Monsoon winds shift, plains grazing is done,
herds move westward, once again,
columns swell, drawn to distant rain,
weaving like smoke through stone-dry grass.

Hoofprints linger in sleeping grass.

In late spring, the large herbivores of the great migration move toward new food sources near the small lakes, grasses, and woodlands of the western Serengeti ecosystem.

Siringet—from the Maasai language: endless.

Every form of life on the Serengeti is linked, one to another, in an intricate web. The verses on each page of this book are linked together in a form I derived from an East African, Swahili poem form with Arabic origins, the utendi.

The utendi is a four-line stanza, or verse. Each line usually has eight syllables but not always an exact number of strong beats. Most of my lines are eight syllables long, but sometimes seven or nine syllables sounded better in English. In the utendi, the first three lines rhyme with each other. The last line ends with a refrain, which is a word or rhyme that is repeated at the end of each stanza. The stanzas in this book are linked to each other by this repeated pattern and by the final word in each stanza, "grass," the food source linking all of the animals to the Serengeti Plain.

Readers will notice that I use partial rhyme for the first three lines of every stanza. Instead of rhyming "mark" with "park" (an example of a perfect rhyme), I rhymed "mark" with "flick," which is a partial rhyme using the same ending consonant with a different vowel sound before it. To my ear, this softer rhyme sounds more like the rhymes used in the utendi.

The early traditional Swahili utendi addressed serious subjects and shared wisdom on how to live a good life in the world. If the Serengeti is to remain an endless plain of grass supporting its intricately beautiful web of life, then we humans must live our best lives in support and stewardship of the Serengeti, one of the greatest ecosystems on our Earth.

Serengeti Glossary

aardvark (*Orycteropus afer*)—a sharp-clawed, nocturnal, burrowing mammal native to Africa, south of the Sahara Desert, that eats termites and ants

antelope—a general term for one of several horned mammals belonging to the family Bovidae found in Africa, North America, and Asia; an antelope chews cud like a sheep or cow

black mamba (*Dendroaspis polylepis*)—a fast, long, venomous snake native to southern and eastern Africa

browser—a plant-eater that gets nutrition and water from the leaves, buds, and fruit of trees and shrubs

burrow—a hole or tunnel in the ground that provides shelter for an animal

carnivore—an animal that eats the flesh of other animals

carrion—the dead or decomposing flesh of an animal

cattle egret (*Bubulcus ibis*)—a medium-sized white bird related to herons that is found in Africa, the Americas, and other parts of the world; it is often seen eating insects disturbed by grazing and browsing mammals

cheetah (*Acinonyx jubatus jubatus*)—the Serengeti-dwelling subspecies of a large, spotted cat found almost exclusively in Africa that can run at great speeds for short distances to chase prey; Earth's fastest land animal

cud—food brought back up from the stomach of a grazer like a sheep or cow to be chewed again and broken down further, releasing more nutrients

dik-dik (*Madoqua kirkii*)—a southern African antelope browser about the size of a toy poodle

dung beetle (*Scarabaeidae species*)—a type of scarab beetle found on all continents except Antarctica that eats animal manure, recycling nutrients into soil

ecosystem—a community of organisms and their interactions with each other and with the nonliving parts of their environment

golden jackal (*Canis aureus*)—a medium-sized omnivore related to dogs that is found in northern and eastern Africa, the Middle East, Europe, and Asia

grazer—a plant-eater with a diet of grasses; a grazer must drink additional water

herb—grass or other soft-stemmed plant

herbivore—an animal that eats only plant material

kopje—an outcropping of boulders in the Serengeti Plain

larva—the newly hatched form of an insect, which can look quite different from its adult form; two or more are called larvae

Maasai giraffe (*Giraffa camelopardalis tippelskirchi*)—the Serengeti-dwelling subspecies of an African browsing mammal that feeds on the leaves and buds of trees and shrubs; Earth's tallest mammal

mammal—a furred or hairy vertebrate animal that makes internal heat to maintain constant body temperature and produces milk to nourish its infants; nearly all mammals give birth to live young.

manure—the digestive waste produced and eliminated by animals and rich in undigested nutrients

migration—a mass movement of a group of animals from one habitat to another for food, water, or reproduction

monsoon—a seasonal wind bringing heavy rains

mound-building termite—a general term for an insect living in large social groups that build tall, complex, mud-tunnel nests and feed nocturnally on grass and/or wood; termites are ecosystem engineers that restructure habitat and recycle nutrients back into soil

nectar—a sugary liquid that is produced by plants; nectar attracts pollinators

nutrient—a fundamental substance an organism needs to function and grow

omnivore—an animal that eats a varied diet including plants and animals

parasite—an animal or plant that lives on or in a host organism, causing varying degrees of harm

plain—open grassland

plains zebra *(Equus quagga)*—a grazing horse relative found in southeastern Africa that can digest large amounts of less nutritious plants like older grass stems and blades

pollinator—an animal such as an insect, bird, or bat that carries pollen grains from the male part of a flower (the anther) to the female part (the stigma), helping the plant make fruit or seeds.

predator—a carnivorous animal that kills and eats live animals

raptor—a predatory bird that primarily hunts vertebrate animals

red-billed oxpecker *(Buphagus erythrorhynchus)*—a perching bird in southern and eastern Africa about the size of a red-winged blackbird

rock hyrax *(rocavia capensis matschiei)*—the Serengeti-dwelling subspecies of a small African and Middle-Eastern mammal the size of a gopher; it is more closely related to elephants than to rodents; this herbivorous grazer and browser will sometimes eat insects

scavenger—an animal that eats the flesh of dead animals killed by a predator or dead by other natural causes

scrum—a group of vultures gathering at the site of a dead animal

• **secretary bird** *(Sagittarius serpentarius)*—a tall, long-legged raptor with quills angling out from its head that hunts for prey on the ground in Africa south of the Sahara Desert; also known as a "marching eagle"

Serengeti Plain—the open grassland portion of the larger Serengeti National Park, which is part of the even larger Serengeti ecosystem that includes adjacent game reserves and conservation areas in northwestern Tanzania and southwestern Kenya

spotted hyena *(Crocuta crocuta)*—a large, predatory and scavenging mammal related to cats, found in Africa; has strong molar teeth and jaws that can crack and chew bone, and digests nearly all parts of its prey animals

stowaboard—an informal synonym for stowaway; a passenger riding on a ship without permission of the captain

subspecies—a smaller group of organisms within a species that has recognizable physical and genetic differences but can still have offspring with others in the larger species group, and indicated by a third name in an organism's scientific name after genus and species

Thomson's gazelle *(Eudorcas thomsonii)*—a small, browsing antelope found in East Africa

vertebrate—a member of the large group (subphylum) of animals that typically have an internal skeleton with a backbone

waste paper flower *(Cycnium tubulosum)*—the flower of low-growing plants that live as partial parasites, taking water and minerals from the roots of short grasses; also called tissue paper flower or vlei ink-flower

western white-bearded wildebeest *(Connochaetes taurinus mearnsi)*—the Serengeti-dwelling subspecies of the blue wildebeest, a large, stocky, grass-eating antelope found in southern and eastern Africa; also called gnu

whistling thorn acacia *(Vachellia drepanolobium)*—a common thorn tree in East Africa that bears seedpods; specialized ants protect leaves from browsing animals and benefit from the tree's nectar, sheltering in hollow bases of thorns that whistle in the wind once the ants have moved on

•• **white-backed vulture** *(Gyps africanus)*—a large, scavenging raptor that glides in circles on warm air currents called thermals and can locate animal carcasses from great distances

• Endangered
•• Critically endangered
IUCN Red List of Threatened Species accessed 1 Sept 2021

Serengeti Stewardship

Serengeti National Park in Tanzania was named a protected World Heritage Site by the United Nations Educational, Scientific and Cultural Organization (UNESCO) in 1981. The park is at the heart of the larger Serengeti-Mara ecosystem that stretches from the Ngorongoro Conservation Area in Tanzania to the Maasai Mara National Reserve in southern Kenya. Within this vast ecosystem, the seasonal migration of nearly two million wildebeests, zebras, and gazelles creates a moving food web that links migrants and residents across grassland, woodland, rocky kopje, and river habitats.

We humans have been migrants and residents in the Serengeti-Mara ecosystem throughout our history. Rising local *and* global populations challenge the ecosystem's ability to maintain balance. In Tanzania and Kenya, as local towns grow, so does the need to raise crops and livestock at the edges of protected areas. Greater numbers of tourists visiting the Serengeti and other protected reserves add to demand for food services and transportation. These human activities compete with wildlife for precious water resources and grazing lands. Livestock diseases may infect wild animals. Pressure to build roads across critical wildlife corridors and the poaching of wild animals challenge governments and organizations working to protect the ecosystem. At the same time, excluding indigenous peoples who have stewarded this area for centuries—notably the Maasai pastoralists who gave Serengeti its name—impacts their human rights, cultural rights, livelihoods, and survival. And on a global scale, human-induced climate change is disrupting the monsoon rainfall pattern that drives the great migration cycle.

The Serengeti-Mara is one of the most productive and biodiverse ecosystems on Earth. Through our combined best efforts in all responsibilities of stewardship and partnership we can help the Serengeti and its larger ecosystem remain "endless" for its inhabitants, neighbors, and worldwide visitors for millennia to come.

Serengeti Watch

serengetiwatch.org

This international nongovernmental organization (NGO) builds worldwide awareness and financial support for local programs in the greater Serengeti ecosystem, working with its Tanzanian nonprofit organization partner, the Serengeti Preservation Foundation. Initiatives include conservation education for teachers and students, women's empowerment, clean water, tree-planting, and radio programming produced with help from UNESCO.

Serengeti Watch also sponsors "Friends of Serengeti," a designation awarded to member tourism companies promoting responsible and sustainable tourism.

The Elephant Map Project

redstonestudios.com/elephant

Though the African Elephant (*Loxodonta africana*) is not featured in this text, it is a keystone species that helps shape its Serengeti-Mara ecosystem. By trampling paths, widening watering holes, dispersing seeds in its dung, and munching acacia saplings, this mixed grazer-browser engineers and maintains the grassland system upon which the great migration is based. Custom mapmaker Constance Brown invited me to contribute an elephant poem to "Elephant Map Project," a detailed educational conservation map depicting the decrease of this endangered species* over time. Proceeds from this stunning map poster support baby elephants orphaned through poaching.

*IUCN Red List of Threatened Species accessed 1 Sept 2021

For Further Reading

Kennedy, Adam Scott and Vicki Kennedy. 2014. *Animals of the Serengeti and Ngorongoro Conservation Area.* Princeton University Press. New Jersey. A concise, photo-illustrated guidebook containing identifying and fascinating behavioral information about mammals and reptiles in the Serengeti ecosystem.

Montgomery, Sy. 2019. *The Magnificent Migration.* Houghton Mifflin Harcourt. New York. An information-rich journal that presents observations and photos as a field notebook, bringing readers right into the author's quest to witness the great wildebeest migration in the Serengeti-Mara ecosystem.

Norton, Boyd. 2011. *Serengeti: The Eternal Beginning.* Fulcrum Publishing. Boulder, CO. A lush, photo-illustrated history through present-day challenges in the Serengeti-Mara ecosystem including its geology, human inhabitants, animals, and the great migration.

Acknowledgments

"So, we have spent two days and a lifetime in Serengeti—an ocean of grass . . ."

I have carried a deep impression of the Serengeti Plain in my heart for over twenty years. I am honored to share my reverence for such a remarkable place through the verses on these pages. For our family visit to the Serengeti I thank my sister-in-law, Dr. Susan Hirsch of George Mason University, for her generous invitation.

Many thanks to Dr. Cole Gilbert of Cornell University for the benefit of his knowledge and experience of the Serengeti ecosystem, for his review of the body of the manuscript and glossary, and for his fine poetic ear.

To Peachtree Publishing Company, my dear writing partners and friends, so much appreciation for your critical feedback and support. And to my family, an endless plain of love and thanks.

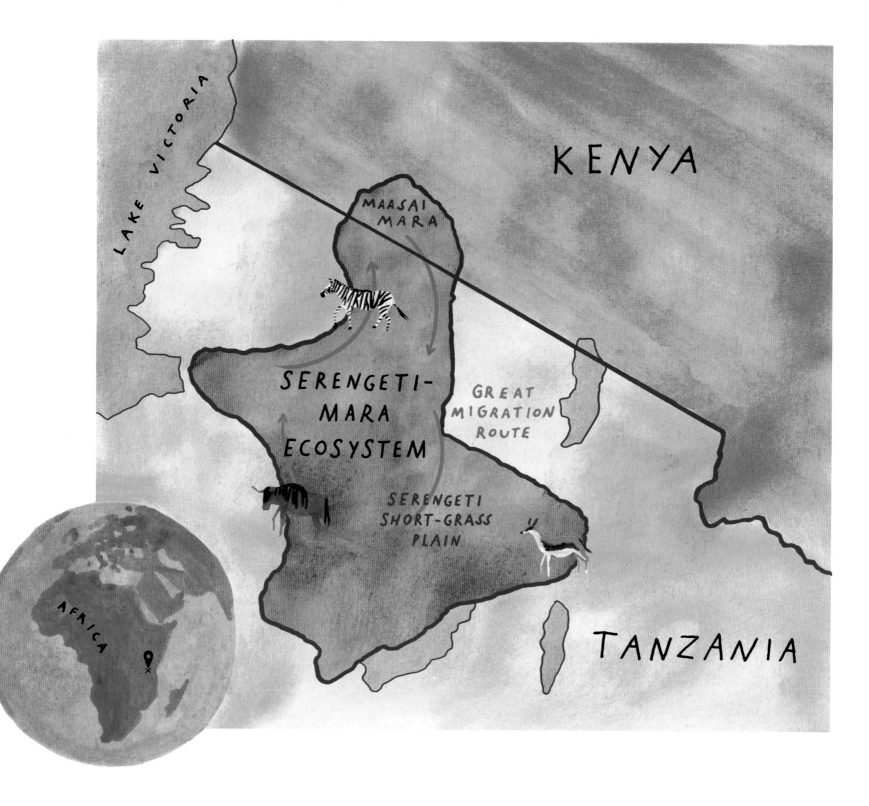

KENYA

LAKE VICTORIA

MAASAI
MARA

SERENGETI-
MARA
ECOSYSTEM

GREAT
MIGRATION
ROUTE

SERENGETI
SHORT-GRASS
PLAIN

AFRICA

TANZANIA